HUMAN BODY   ANIMAL BODIES

BODY PARTS

Izzi Howell

WAYLAND
www.waylandbooks.co.uk

First published in Great Britain in 2017 by Wayland
Copyright © Hodder and Stoughton Limited, 2017

All rights reserved
ISBN: 978 1 5263 0676 0
10 9 8 7 6 5 4 3 2 1

Wayland
An imprint of Hachette Children's Group
Part of Hodder & Stoughton
Carmelite House
50 Victoria Embankment
London EC4Y 0DZ

An Hachette UK Company
www.hachette.co.uk
www.hachettechildrens.co.uk

A catalogue for this title is available from
the British Library
Printed and bound in China

Produced for Wayland by
White-Thomson Publishing Ltd
www.wtpub.co.uk
Editor: Izzi Howell
Design: Clare Nicholas

Picture credits:
iStock: EcoPic 13bl, Squaredpixels 18, Antagain 21r; Shutterstock: elephant *cover l*, hand *cover r*, Sabphoto title page and 15t, Africa Studio 4, Nejron Photo 5t, Kuttelvaserova Stuchelova 5b, Halfbottle 6, wildestanimal 7t, hagit berkovich 7bl, Yevhenii Chulovskyi 7br, Blend Images 8, Andrew M. Allport 9t, bikeriderlondon 9b, In Green 10, Anneka 11t, Zoltan Major 11c, nattanan726 11b, Gelpi 12, clearviewstock 13t, FotoRequest 13br, Patrick Foto 14tl, all_about_people 14tr, David Alexander Stein 14b, Kletr 15b, photka and tratong 16–17t, john michael evan potter 16b, Giedriius 17bl, Anton_Ivanov 17br, Dejan Stanisavljevic 19tl, Coffeemill 19tr, anat chant 19bl, Anan Kaewkhammul 19br, Jorg Hackemann 20, nbiebach 21tl, Iakov Filimonov 21bl.
All design elements from Shutterstock.

Should there be any inadvertent omission, please apply to the publisher for rectification.

The author, Izzi Howell, is a writer and editor specialising in children's educational publishing.

Contents

Human and animal bodies

Human bodies and animal bodies look different. However, we have some of the same body parts.

Look at the pictures. Which body parts come in pairs?

hair

head

neck

skin

hand

toes

arm

fingers

a human

leg

foot

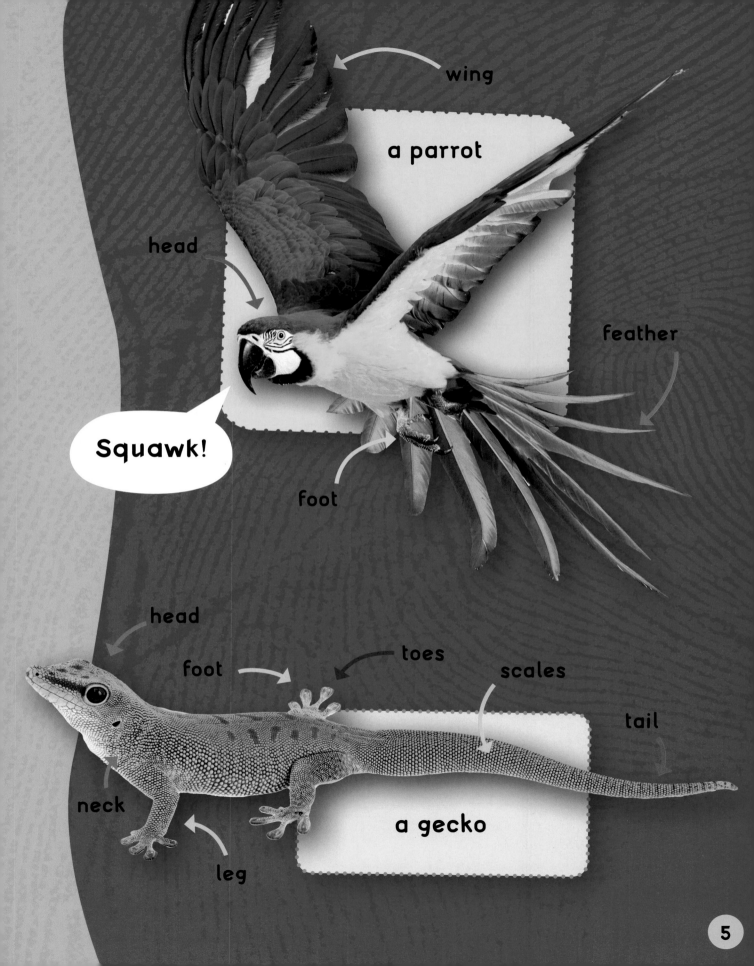

Head

Humans have two eyes, a mouth and a nose on their face. Our face is at the front of our head. We have ears on the sides of our head.

mouth

eye

nose

ear

I see you!

eye

mouth

a hammerhead shark

Animals sometimes have their eyes, ears, nose and mouth in different places on their head.

a snail

ear

eye

nose

a fennec fox

mouth

eyes

Neck

Our neck allows us to turn and move our head. Humans can't move their head very far in any direction.

Owls can nearly turn their head all the way round. They can't move their eyes like humans can so they move their head instead.

Yum!

Giraffes have very long necks. This helps them to eat leaves from the tops of trees.

Skin

Skin protects our body. It stops germs from getting inside.

smooth, soft human skin

Animal skin looks and feels different to human skin.

moist tree frog skin

shiny red snapper scales

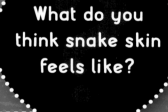

What do you think snake skin feels like?

hard crocodile scales

Hair and fur

Long, thick hair grows on human heads.
Short, fine hair grows all over our body.

Roar!

a tiger

Some animals are covered in thick fur. The colour of their fur helps them to hide in the wild.

stripy fur in long grass

white fur in snow

beige fur in sandy soil

a snowshoe hare

meerkats

Can you think of another animal with white fur?

Arms, wings and fins

Humans can bend their arms at the elbow.
We can move our arms **up**...   **across**...

common egrets

and **out**.

Fish move
their fins to
change direction
in the water. Their
tail fin pushes
them forwards.

a clownfish

Birds have wings instead of
arms. When most birds flap their
wings, they fly up into the sky.

15

Hands

Inside human hands, there are lots of tiny bones. They allow us to move our fingers in different ways.

waving

Ouch!

pinching

Animals hold and carry things with a different part of their body.

an African elephant's trunk

writing

holding

pointing

Yum!

a sea eagle's claws

a spider monkey's tail

Legs

Humans stand on two legs. We use our legs to walk, run, skip and jump.

Some animals have two legs. Others have four, six, eight or many more.

a flamingo

a tarantula

a deer

a centipede

How many legs do you think a centipede has?

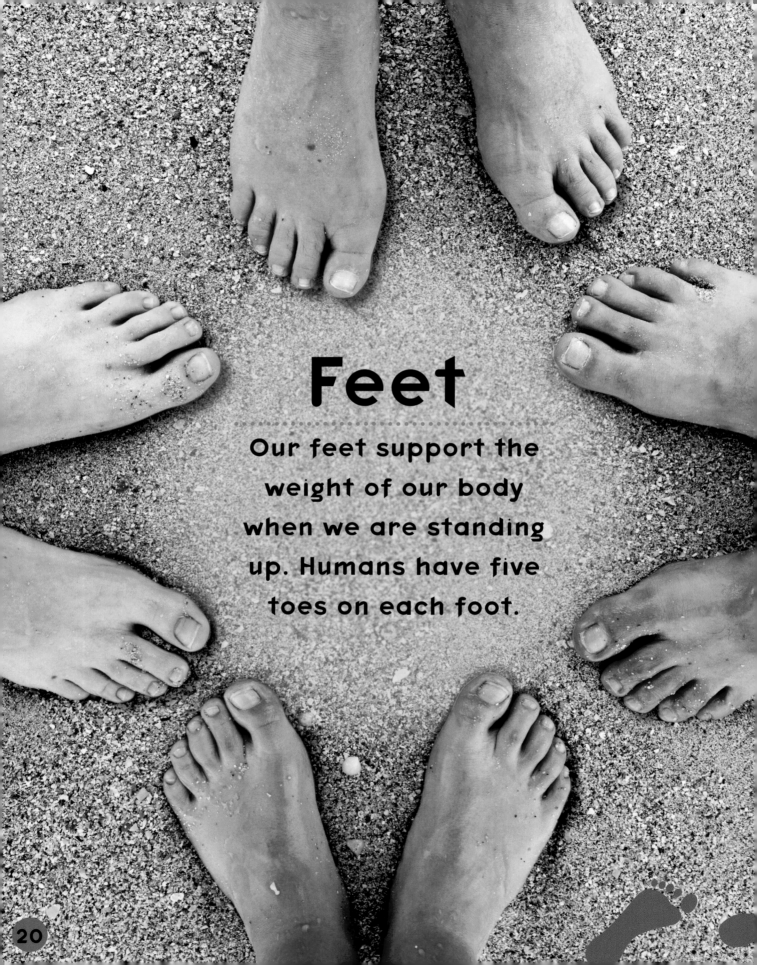

Feet

Our feet support the
weight of our body
when we are standing
up. Humans have five
toes on each foot.

Some animals have webbed feet. Others have paws and hooves.

a cat's paw

a duck's webbed foot

a Bactrian camel's hoof

Human and animal classification

Mammals

African elephant

Bactrian camel

cat

deer

fennec fox

giraffe

human

meerkat

snowshoe hare

spider monkey

tiger

FEATURES

two or four legs

fur or skin

Birds

common egret

duck

flamingo

owl

parrot

sea eagle

FEATURES

wings

two legs

feathers

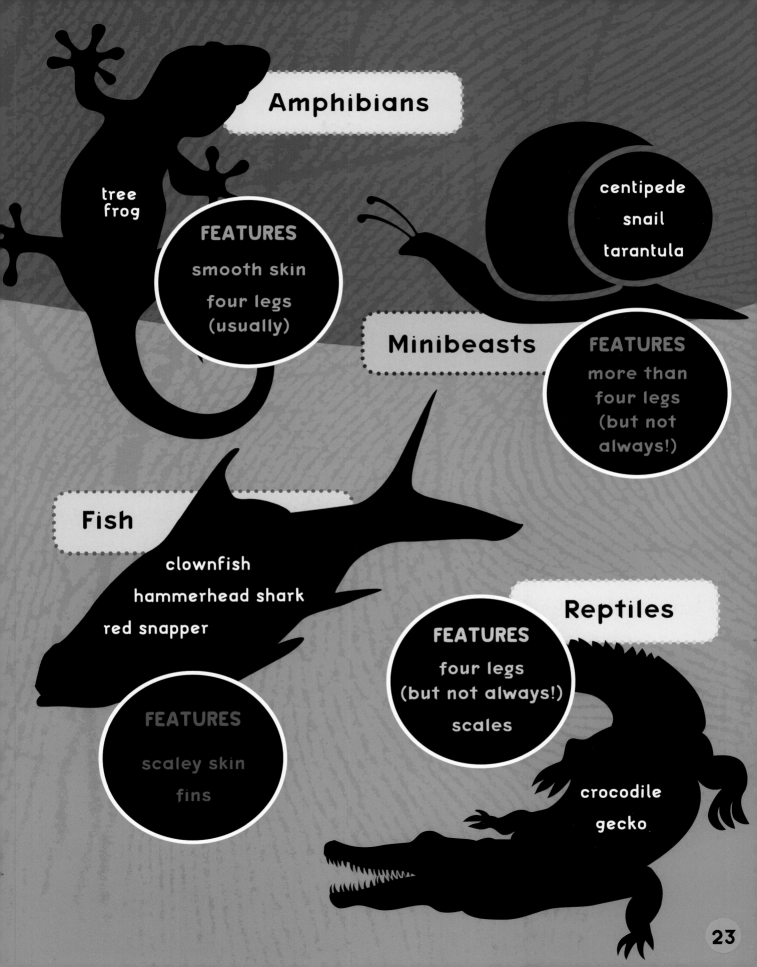

Amphibians

tree frog

FEATURES

smooth skin

four legs (usually)

centipede

snail

tarantula

Minibeasts

FEATURES

more than four legs (but not always!)

Fish

clownfish

hammerhead shark

red snapper

Reptiles

FEATURES

four legs (but not always!)

scales

FEATURES

scaley skin

fins

crocodile

gecko

Index

Answers

p4 — Arms, hands, legs, feet and wings
p13 — Polar bear, arctic fox
p19 — Between 14 and 177 pairs of legs

HUMAN BODY ANIMAL BODIES

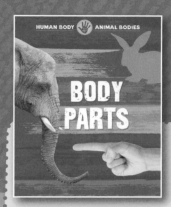

978 1 5263 0676 0

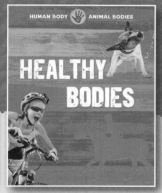

978 1 5263 0678 4

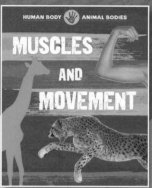

978 1 5263 0680 7

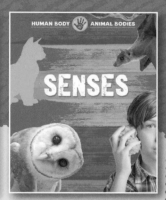

978 1 5263 0682 1

BODY PARTS

Human and animal bodies
Head
Neck
Skin
Hair and fur
Arms, wings and fins
Hands
Legs
Feet
Human and animal classification

HEALTHY BODIES

Feeling healthy
Breathing
Diet
Animal diets
Water
Sleeping
Exercise
Keeping warm
Staying clean
Healthy humans and animals

MUSCLES AND MOVEMENT

Muscles
Bones
Exoskeletons
Walking
Running
Jumping
Swimming
Flying
Slithering
Human and animal movement

SENSES

What are senses?
Sight
Looking around
Hearing
Taste
Different tastes
Touch
Smell
Special senses
Human and animal senses

WAYLAND
www.waylandbooks.co.uk